AMERICA'S

Published by Gallery Books
A Division of W H Smith Publishers Inc.
112 Madison Avenue
New York, New York 10016

Produced by
Bison Books Corp.
17 Sherwood Place
Greenwich, CT 06830

ISBN 0-8317-7912-8

Printed in Hong Kong

1 2 3 4 5 6 7 8 9 10

SOUTHWEST

TEXT   THOMAS G AYLESWORTH
VIRGINIA L AYLESWORTH

PHOTOGRAPHY   JERRY SIEVE

DESIGN   MIKE ROSE

GALLERY BOOKS
An imprint of W.H. Smith Publishers Inc.
112 Madison Avenue
New York, New York 10016

A Bison Book

Note from the photographer

The photographs in this book were made with cameras ranging in size from 35mm to 8x10, with the majority being in the 4x5 format. For the 4x5 work I use lenses of 75, 135, 250 and 500mm focal lengths. Filters are rarely used except for occasional polarization.

Being aware of light and its dramatic effects is my main concern when approaching a subject. At times, split second decisions must be made to take advantage of the interplay between light and landscape, making a mental preconception of the image helpful. Knowledge of light is a skill learned through experience that I feel is especially important when photographing the southwestern states.

Acknowledgments

The authors and publisher would like to thank the following people who have helped in the preparation of this book: Mike Rose, who designed it; Barbara Paulding Thrasher, who edited it; Mary R Raho, who did the picture research.

Photo Credits

All photographs by Jerry Sieve, with the following exceptions:
M A C Miles: 126
The Stockhouse, Inc: Scott Berner (83, 84, 85); K Cole (102, 103, 124, 125); Chris Jones (93); Richard Stockton (100-01)

3/6 Morning sun breaks through storm clouds at Dead Horse Point State Park in Utah.

PREFACE

America's Southwest is defined as much by its Spanish and Indian cultural heritage as it is by its unique geological and geographical parameters. A dramatic, even unearthly, appeal marks much of the southwestern landscape, from twisting arches of red sedimentary rock to sculpted and seemingly endless desert dunes, and from jagged mountain peaks receding in blue haze to waterfalls tumbling over red cliffs.

Similarly, the cities and towns of the Southwest—from Acoma Pueblo in New Mexico to San Antonio in Texas to Las Vegas in Nevada—have a distinctive flavor, a curious blend of ancient and modern, cosmopolitan and provincial. The essence of the Southwest region is captured in these landscapes and towns, which in turn define the region covered in this volume. Centered around Arizona and New Mexico, the Southwest encompasses western Texas, southwestern Colorado, southern Utah and the southern tips of Nevada and California.

Although much of it was once consigned to the Indians as useless, the Southwest is today a rich and highly unusual region. Where Spanish *conquistadores* once vainly searched for gold, fabulous bonanzas of oil and gas now flow from the ground. Where hard-riding cowboys once herded cattle on the long drives, space scientists now push the frontiers of technology toward a new age. Huge cities dot the landscape where once there was a wilderness.

This does not mean that the wide open spaces are disappearing. The magnificent vistas in which rock formations 50 miles off seem near at hand are still there. Towering mountains fringed with thick ponderosa pine and aspen forests rise within sight of unbelievably deep canyons. Jagged, twisted lava beds spewed out by now-extinct volcanoes scar terrain that edges flower-bedecked meadows. Mesquite groves crowd spiny cacti while palm leaves fan backyard patios. Such earth-moving rivers as the Colorado and Rio Grande—plus hundreds of sky-blue lakes—water some of the most arid landscape in North America. Add to this the mesas, the deserts, the cities, and one finds that the Southwest is truly one of the most varied places on earth.

People have lived in the Southwest since before the birth of Christ, going back to the Stone Age Indians of New Mexico and the Hohokam Desert Indian Tribes in Arizona—who may have lived there 20,000 years ago. There are well-constructed cliff dwellings—houses, apartments and whole towns—in New Mexico that may date back that far. About 2000 years ago there were basket-making Indians, and by 700 AD the Pueblo period was under way.

The white man learned of the area much later, beginning in the sixteenth century. Juan Cabrillo discovered San Diego Bay in the early part of that century. In 1539, the Spaniard, Fray Friar Marcos de Niza, made a preliminary exploration into what is now New Mexico and Arizona, and Francisco Vasquez Coronado came in search of the fabled Seven Cities of Cibola. Of course he did not find those seven wealthy cities, but he did claim the whole region for the Spanish Crown. The first settlement made by the Spaniards was in New Mexico in 1598, and Santa Fe became the capital of this new Spanish colony in 1610. As might be expected, Roman Catholic missionaries came with the explorers to convert the Indians.

Hernando de Soto also explored in the Southwest, and the Indians, mostly

Apache and Navajo, were pretty much subdued, but settlement of the region was slow. Then a Frenchman, Cavelier, established a town in Texas, Fort Saint Louis, in 1685. Even though the town was destroyed by the Indians two years later, the Spanish became alarmed by the French intrusion, and sent in more expeditions and missionaries, who began to build forts and missions in the Southwest.

In 1718 came the founding of the Mission San Antonio de Valero, which became present-day San Antonio. To the West, Spanish settlement began in southern California in 1769 and continued for almost 50 years, resulting in 21 missions, each about a day's ride from the next, running up to San Francisco, the beginnings of such southwestern cities as San Diego and Los Angeles and the naming in Spanish of almost every natural feature in the southern half of California. The Spanish colonists traveled up and down the state over a Spanish road called El Camino Real (The King's Highway). This is a highway which, in places, still retains its original name, although officially, on maps, it is actually US Highway 101.

Of the seven states or parts of states in the Southwest, Texas achieved official statehood status in 1845. It was followed by California (1850), Nevada (1864), Colorado (1876), Utah (1896), New Mexico (1912) and Arizona (1912).

Today the Southwest region is a combination of the rough and ready with the truly cosmopolitan. Industry and agriculture and natural resources have brought in people from every part of North America, as well as from overseas. It is a land of education, with outstanding institutions of higher education. It is a land of museums and scientific establishments. It is a wide-open land of outdoor sports—hunting, fishing, horseback riding, boating.

The natural beauty of America's Southwest includes cacti blooming in the desert dusk, canyon gorges cutting a fanciful maze in the red earth, the lights of Phoenix twinkling at night before a mountain backdrop, aspen leaves floating on the surface of a trickling stream, or fantastic formations contorting rock and defying gravity. With its Indian, Spanish and American pioneer heritage, with its abundance of wild beauty and with its wealth of resources, the Southwest is one of America's most richly diverse and fascinating regions.

Thomas G Aylesworth

Virginia L Aylesworth

CANYONS, BUTTES AND MESAS

Nature has endowed the Southwest with an abundance of canyons, buttes and mesas. And each of them represents a period of formation that must have been millions of years in length. One of the most outstanding features of a geologically young river is the cutting of a V-shaped valley when the river is still above its base level. As the river continues to erode its channel, sometimes the downcutting occurs much faster than the walls of its valley are eroded by the weathering of wind and rain. The result is a narrow, steep-walled valley, called a canyon or a gorge.

One of the mightiest of these canyons is, of course, the Grand Canyon, which is located in northern Arizona on the Colorado River Plateau. Here the land is covered with deeply cut crevices and high peaks ranging from black to red, lavender, brown and sand in color. The canyon is as much as 18 miles wide and about a mile deep—truly a magnificent sight.

Buttes and mesas, on the other hand, are formed when an area of rock, resistant to most of the effects of wind and water erosion, lies on top of softer minerals. On all sides, the more erodible rock is worn away, leaving the resistant rock, which stretches skyward, forming a mesa. A butte is merely a small mesa.

One of the more unearthly mesas in the Southwest is Acoma, 357 feet above the surrounding plain about 12 miles south of the road between Grants and Albuquerque, New Mexico. On top is an Indian pueblo that may be the oldest continuously inhabited town in the US—perhaps dating to the year 600. It is eerily quiet, with more buildings than are needed for its populace (numbering about a dozen). There is no electricity and water must be carried up the sheer face of the mesa, where some of it is used by inhabitants to chill soft drinks. This creative blending of old and new, traditional and modern, characterizes much of the Southwest. Here, the pueblo dwellings signify a connection with an ancient world, as their architecture suggests a harmony between man and nature.

15 An awe-inspiring view on an August morning from Toroweap Point in the Grand Canyon of Arizona. Every minute of the day the light changes the details of color and form of this magnificent spectacle. Sunrises and sunsets are particularly superb.

16/17 A morning view from the North Rim of the Grand Canyon. The Spanish explorer Cardenas was the first white man to see this canyon of the Colorado River in 1540. Naturally he and his party were unable to cross it, so they promptly left.

18/19 A sunset view from Moran Point on the South Rim of the Grand Canyon. In 1857 American Lieutenant Joseph Ives predicted, 'It is altogether valueless.... Ours has been the first and will doubtless be the last party of whites to visit this profitless locality.'

20 The graphic shapes of the Mitten Buttes at sunrise in Monument Valley Tribal Park in Arizona—a park that covers 96,000 acres on the Navajo Reservation in the northeastern part of the state. The tribal council maintains a tourist center here.

21 Autumn adds a touch more color to the already colorful Red Rock Crossing below Cathedral Rock near Sedona, Arizona. A feature of the area is the uniquely colored red sandstone, which indicates that the region was once under the sea.

22 A young prickly pear cactus among the sandstone patterns of Snow Canyon State Park, Utah. The park encompasses a flat-bottomed gorge cut into multicolored Navajo sandstone, plus massive erosional forms, and is located near St George.

23 The Sands of Time rock formation located in the spectacular Monument Valley, near Kayenta, Arizona. The area around this small town offers some of the most memorable sightseeing in the state, and the great tinted monoliths are spectacular.

24/25 A view of the Great Goosenecks of the San Juan River in the San Juan State Reserve near Mexican Hat, Utah. The gorge is 1500 feet deep, and the water follows a path five miles long to advance the river one mile.

26/27 The Santa Elena Canyon along the Rio Grande. The cliff on the right is in the Big Bend National Park in Texas, and the cliff on the left is in Mexico. The sheer rock walls of the canyons here may reach a height of 1500 feet.

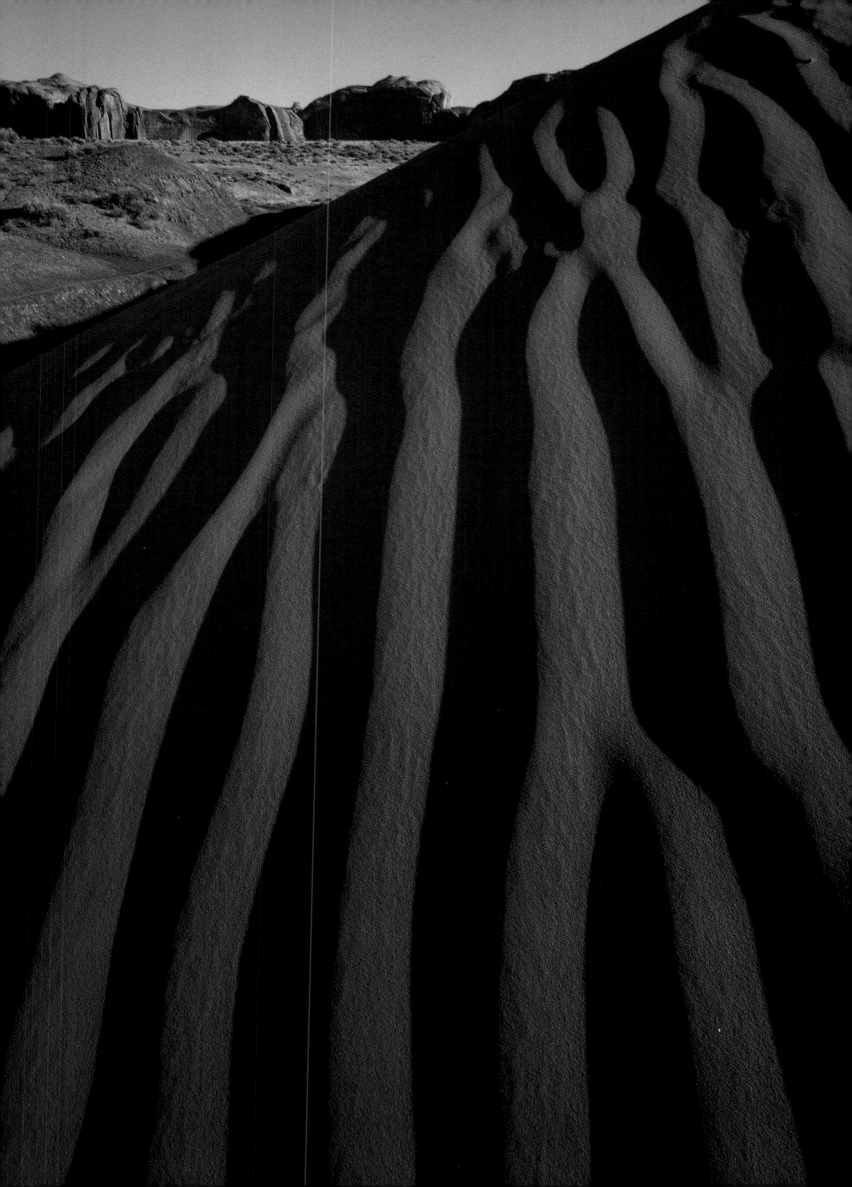

28/29 Day's end in Golden Canyon in Death Valley National Monument, California. The canyon offers a display of color ranging from deep purple to rich gold. Death Valley was named when a party of gold hunters took a short cut here and were lost in 1849.

30 The Tsegi Overlook at sunrise in Canyon de Chelly National Monument in Arizona. The smooth sandstone walls of the canyon extend upwards as much as 1000 feet above the nearly flat sand bottom. Pueblo Indians were settled here more than a thousand years ago.

31 Mooney Falls in Havasu Canyon in the Grand Canyon National Park in Arizona. In addition to the spectacular scenery, the park is home to some 220 different species of birds, 67 species of mammals, 25 species of reptiles and six species of amphibians.

32 The sunset color highlights the pinnacles below Point Supreme in the Cedar Breaks National Monument in Utah. The Monument is about four miles long and two and one-half miles wide and is located at an elevation of about 10,000 feet.

33 Another evening view of the area below Point Supreme in the Cedar Breaks National Monument. The rock formations, although fewer than in the famous Bryce Canyon National Park, are considerably more vivid and varied in color.

34/35 East Temple in Zion National Park, Utah. Zion Canyon is a deep, narrow, multicolored, vertically walled chasm with other canyons branching from it like fingers. On the sides are massive rock formations in awe-inspiring colors— many are described as temples.

36 A delicate arch in Arches National Park, Utah. In the distance are the La Sal Mountains. The park covers some 144 square miles of red rock terrain, with 88 stone arches and numerous fancifully shaped formations and objects.

37 Sunrise colors the area below Sunrise Point in Bryce Canyon National Park in Utah. The 56 square miles of this park enclose a land of cream, pink and red spires, domes, temples and figures, including numerous niches and fantastic rock formations.

DESERTS

As the prevailing westerly winds sweep in from the Pacific Ocean over the western coast of the United States, they soon come in contact with the Sierra Nevada Mountains. The high slopes of these mountains cause the moist winds to rise, become cooler and, as a consequence, lose much of their moisture before they get over the towering peaks. That means that the winds are quite dry east of the mountains, very little rain falls on this area, and deserts are formed.

Deserts can be foreboding places—hot, waterless and stark. But at times they can be beautiful places, with their wealth of blossoms, their quiet and ever-shifting sand dunes, the diversity of their animal life and their stately cactus plants. Actually, the American desert is not sterile. Most places there that can be irrigated can produce surprisingly large crop yields. There is the additional virtue of their having very hot summers, but mild winters, with warm days.

Some of the most beautiful areas in the United States are the deserts—and most of them are in the Southwest. Death Valley in California contains the lowest point in the United States—282 feet below sea level. Yet on a highway in southeastern California one can look east to this blazing heart of Death Valley near Badwater, and west to the snowy crest of Mount Whitney, the highest point, at 14,494 feet, in the lower 48 states.

Other deserts in the Southwest have their charms, too. The Sonora Desert is thick with wildlife. The Mojave Desert is a rarity, being located more than 2000 feet above sea level. White Sands features gypsum sand that is soft and cool and fun to roll around on. The Petrified Forest is really a desert that contains the remains of petrified wood and probably was once a vast forest. All

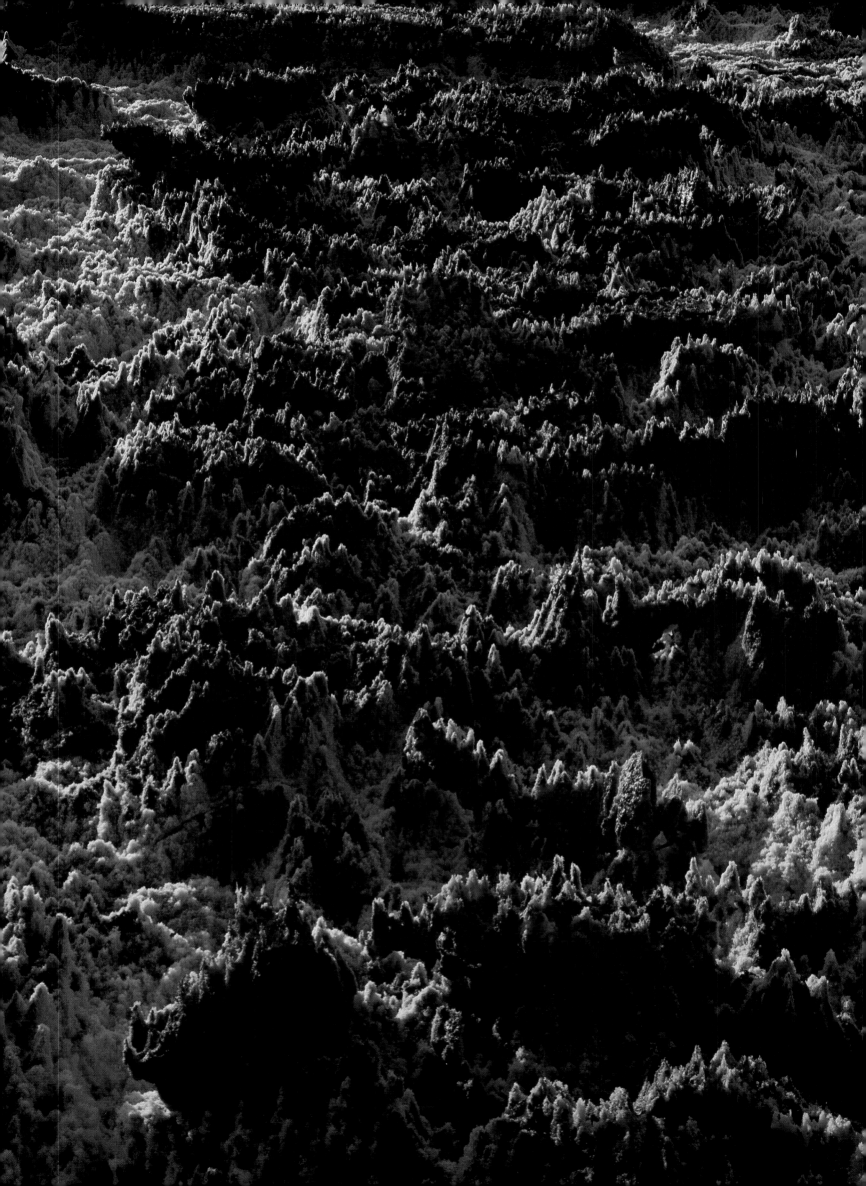

42 A salt formation at 'The Devil's Golf Course' in Death Valley, California. These vast beds of rugged salt crystals were crossed by some of the pioneers who came to California in the mid-nineteenth century—the '49ers.'

43 Caked mud is mute testimony to vanished water in arid country. These are the Mesquite Flat Dunes in Death Valley. This valley is an area of rugged desert, peaks and depressions—3000 square miles of weird and colorful geography.

44/45 Rolling dunes at the White Sands National Monument in New Mexico. Beach sand is usually silica, but this sand comes from gypsum, from which plaster of paris is made. The monument encloses an area of 145,344 acres of this exotic sand.

46 Desert primroses welcome the morning sun in the Kelso Dunes section of the Mojave National Recreation Area in California. This relative of the evening primrose and the fireweed is common in the area.

47 A barrel cactus (foreground) and several tall, stately Saguaro cacti are seen in the desert fog north of Cave Creek in the Tonto National Forest near Payson, Arizona, an area that has provided the locale for many cowboy movies.

48/49 A winter afternoon in the Blue Mesa area of the Petrified Forest National Park in Arizona. The 93,493 acres of this park contain the most spectacular display of petrified wood in the world, as well as mesas, pinnacles, ledges and canyons.

50 Evening colors in the Petrified Forest National Park in Arizona. This erosion-shaped area, almost devoid of trees, is part of the Chinle formation, a soft shale, clay, marl and sandstone stratum of the Triassic Age.

51 Flowers in the sands of the Valley of Fire State Park in Nevada. The park contains 46,000 acres of red Jurassic sandstone that was formed some 150 million years ago. Indian petroglyphs can be seen throughout the park.

52/53 Various species of cactus grow in the deserts of the southwestern states. The giant Saguaro cactus plants in the background can grow to a height of 50 feet and may live for some 200 years. In April they sprout splendid creamy-white blossoms.

54/55 Stately cacti stretch their arms to the sky during a desert sunset in central Arizona. There are more than 1000 species of cacti and many of them have not been named. Many cactus varieties have beautiful, delicate flowers.

56 The bobcat is a common denizen of the desert. A relatively small animal of 15 to 25 pounds and a length of about three feet, the bobcat (or wildcat) is nocturnal and subsists on small animals including birds, rattlesnakes, mice and rabbits.

57 The Gila monster is usually found in the desert regions of the Southwest, most commonly in Arizona. It is the only poisonous lizard in the United States, but seems to rely on eggs for its main food.

58 Grasses blowing in the White Sands National Monument in New Mexico. These shifting, dazzling white dunes are a challenge to plants and animals. Plants grow root systems as long as 40 feet which anchor them in the constantly moving sands.

59 The star-burst pattern of a Joshua tree in central Arizona. This plant, a member of the Lily family, reaches a maximum height of 38 feet. White blossoms grow in magnificent clusters at the ends of its angular branches.

60/61 Joshua trees with their spring blossoms seen below the Grand Wash Cliffs in northwestern Arizona.

MOUNTAINS AND FORESTS

Most of the mountainous regions of the Southwest are located in what is called the Basin and Range Province. This is an area of complex rocks with many small mountain ranges and with sedimentary rock beds in the basins between the ranges. The ranges extend roughly north and south. This province includes western Utah, all of Nevada, and portions of California, Arizona, New Mexico and Texas. The western part of southern California belongs in the Pacific Ranges. This province consists of two chains of mountains with a lowland trough between them, extending from Mexico to the Alaskan Peninsula.

In addition to the vast number of mountains, the Southwest contains forests of all sorts— deciduous and coniferous— that contain sky-blue lakes and rushing rivers and streams. More than a score of vast national forests can be found there, and the region boasts countless state parks, state forests and state recreational areas that offer many kinds of outdoor recreation to the visitor.

The mountains and forests of the Southwest seem to have been created for lovers of all seasons and sports. The many species of birds are a delight to the birdwatcher and their songs can be mesmerizing to the casual listener. The streams and lakes provide some of the finest fishing. The waters are ideal for swimmers, water skiers and waders. The forest and lake shores are just the place for families to picnic.

But there is more. Snowmobiling on pure white trails and skiing on gentle slopes and challenging downhill runs is invigorating. Add to all this the opportunities for mountain climbing, backpacking, hiking, hunting, boating, canoeing, nature walking and camping, and surely the Southwest is the greatest outdoor sport region in North America.

63 A fall sunrise at the Dallas Divide in the Uncompahgre National Forest, with 14,150-foot high Mount Sneffels in the distance. The forest contains over one million acres of wild land with elevations of from 7500 to 14,000 feet.

64/65 Sunrise from the Centella Point in the Chiricahua National Monument in Arizona, looking toward both Mexico and New Mexico. The area contains 17 square miles of picturesque natural rock sculpture and deep, twisting canyons.

66/67 A high country meadow filled with wildflowers. This is a morning scene in the Cedar Breaks National Monument near Cedar City, Utah. At an elevation of some 10,000 feet, the area is in the Markagunt Plateau and is surrounded by Dixie National Forest.

68/69 Sundown along the Senator Highway in the Prescott National Forest near Crown King, Arizona. Parts of the Sycamore Canyon and Pine Mountain Wildernesses are located in this forest, which features mineral deposits and varied vegetation.

70 Summer wildflowers near the East Fork of the Black River in the White Mountains of Arizona. The Black River runs through the San Carlos Indian Reservation and the Apache National Forest in east-central Arizona.

71 Columbines blossom in the Cedar Breaks National Monument in Utah. The columbine has been suggested as the national flower of the United States, since it is found almost everywhere, showing its beautiful flowers from April to July.

72/73 A field of summer wildflowers below the distant cloud-covered peaks of the San Francisco Mountains in Arizona. Many people think of Arizona as being primarily an arid desert, but there are many regions in the state that are lush wildernesses.

74/75 A snowy view of the Wilson Mountains in Colorado. These mountains are part of the Rocky Mountain Chain which covers the middle two-fifths of the state of Colorado. The Colorado Rockies have been called 'The Roof of North America.'

76 Sunset over White Horse Lake in Arizona. This southwestern state has many areas of recreation that boast beautiful natural and man-made lakes where boating, canoeing, swimming, camping and fishing can be enjoyed.

77 Sunset behind the Davis Mountains in the Davis Mountains State Park near Alpine, Texas. One of the features of the area, which is a Hereford cattle center, is the masses of agate and other polishing stones. Orchids, maguey, sotol and cacti abound.

78 The sun's final salute through the sycamore trees in Rucker Canyon, Chiricahua National Monument, near Wilcox, Arizona. The monument contains 17 square miles of picturesque natural rock sculpture and deep, twisting canyons.

79 There are five varieties of tanagers to be found in the United States. In the western mountains the most common species, found in many of the fir, pine, sequoia and redwood forests, is the mountain tanager.

80/81 Golden sunset colors on Sunset Crater, east of Flagstaff, Arizona. More than 1000 years ago, this was the site of volcanic eruptions. Sunset Crater itself is a 1000-foot tall cinder cone in the Sunset Crater National Monument.

CITIES

The cities of the Southwest come in all shapes and sizes—old cities and new cities, large cities and small cities, cosmopolitan cities and homespun cities. And all of them are interesting. One can ride elevators to the top of gleaming glass skyscrapers or one can stroll through an old Mexican plaza, or square. One can attend a rodeo or an opera. One can eat French haute cuisine or ranch barbecued ribs. These are cities for all tastes and proclivities.

Many of these cities started out as Spanish missions or Mexican villages. Santa Fe, New Mexico is one such. Founded by Don Pedro de Peralta in 1610, it boasts a main plaza that takes the visitor back to old Spain, yet the city boasts one of the finest summer opera seasons in the world. San Antonio, Texas, is another. Founded as a mission in 1718 by Fray Antonio de San Buenaventura Olivares and home of the Alamo, the shrine of Texas liberty, it lays claim to one of the better symphony orchestras in the country and is one of the few cities where polo teams bring in crowds.

Many of the other cities of the Southwest started out as settlements of pioneers from the East, and today they still exude an eastern nineteenth-century charm. Founded in 1859, Trinidad, Colorado is always a surprise to motorists traveling from New Mexico through Raton Pass into the city. From the stark frontier look of New Mexico they suddenly come across a town that, with its elm- and maple-lined streets, and its architecture, could be located in the Midwest.

Still other towns are products of modern business and agriculture. Las Vegas, Nevada, and Palm Springs, California come to mind. They reflect the modern world we live in.

But each southwestern City—from Phoenix to Albuquerque, and from Tucson to Santa Fe— has a distinctive charm. And the people who live there are proud of being from the Southwest.

83 Old Town, on the west side of Albuquerque, marks the original settlement of the town in 1706. Built around a Spanish-style plaza, its adobe structures (many of them shops and restaurants) reflect the atmosphere of that period.

84 Another view of the Old Town in Albuquerque. In the background is the Church of San Felipe that possesses an unusual spiral staircase built around a spruce tree. In this section of town the Old Town Fiesta is held each June.

85 Modern downtown Albuquerque—a far cry from its Spanish beginnings. The home of the University of New Mexico, this city has a metropolitan area population of almost a half million, and has a fine reputation in the health care field.

86/87 An evening photograph of the Mansion Club (formerly the Wrigley Mansion) with the skyline of Phoenix and the Sierra Estrella Mountains in the distance. Phoenix, like Albuquerque, is prominent in the health care field, and, as a vacation spot, it is both sophisticated and informal.

88 Looking southeast across Phoenix toward the Papago Buttes in the distance. The city lies on a flat desert surrounded by mountains and irrigated fields of cotton, lettuce, melons, vegetables and groves of oranges, grapefruit, lemons and olives.

89 A display of luminarias at the Desert Botanical Gardens in Phoenix. Luminarias are a southwestern tradition at Christmas time— usually created by placing an inch of sand inside a small paper bag, imbedding a candle in the sand, and lighting the candle.

90/91 Dusk over Phoenix, Arizona from the Pinnacle Peak area. The sun shines practically every day in Phoenix, and almost all the rain is restricted to July and August. Although the average temperature in those months is about 90 degrees, the humidity is low.

92 The Mission San Jose y San Miguel de Aguayo, in San Antonio, Texas, dates back to 1720, and the church is still in use. The church is famous for its stone carvings, including the sacristy window, sometimes referred to as 'Rosa's window.'

93 A scene along the beautiful San Antonio River, with its 'Paseo del Rio,' a 21-block river walk, landscaped with tropical foliage, cobblestone walkways, artistic stairways and arched bridges. Water taxis and paddleboats also ply the waters.

94 'The Strip' in Las Vegas, Nevada. Big, brassy and aglow with neon lighting, the Strip is a round-the-clock, year-round resort where the emphasis is put on fun in its casinos and night clubs, where gambling and entertainment are always available.

95 A couple of Las Vegas casinos that offer
roulette wheels, crap and poker games, faro,
chuckaluck and other games of chance. The
games and the bars are open all day and all
night—365 days in the year. Many places stage
elaborate cabaret shows.

96 Downtown Tucson, Arizona. The second largest city in the state, Tucson has a distinct Spanish flavor and spreads across the floor of an ancient sea. Because of the lack of nearby water, the city has a more desert-like look than Phoenix.

97 The old stands next to the new in Tucson. The city has developed under four flags. The Spanish standard flew over the Presidio of Tucson in 1776, built to withstand Apache attacks. Later it was a part of Mexico, the Confederacy, and the United States.

98 Palm Springs, known as 'America's foremost desert resort,' is well named. In nearby Palm Canyon there are 3000 native palm trees lining a stream bed and magnificent views from either the canyon floor or from points above the canyon.

99 A fountain in Palm Springs, California. The area was discovered in 1774 by a Spanish explorer and named Agua Caliente (hot water). One hundred years later it was the site of a stagecoach stop and a one-store railroad town.

100/101 Santa Fe, New Mexico, is situated on a high rolling tableland dotted with piñon pines and backed by the lofty Sangre de Cristo Mountains. Founded by Spaniards about 1610 on an old Indian pueblo, it is the oldest seat of government in the country.

102 The oldest church in the United States is in
Santa Fe, New Mexico. It is the Mission of San
Miguel of Santa Fe, and its restored adobe walls
house priceless paintings and ornaments. The
church was built in 1610 and is still in use.

103 The famous circular staircase in the Loretto
Chapel in Santa Fe. It was erected without central
support and put together with wooden pegs. This
chapel was built by the sisters of Loretto, the first
religious women to come to New Mexico.

GLIMPSES

The great American Southwest is far more than a collection of canyons, buttes, mesas, deserts, mountains, forests and cities. It is images of people, moments in time, angles of light, sounds and smells that evoke a feeling of place. It is Zuni dancers captivating onlookers with their rhythmic movements, the sanctuary offered within the white walls of a mission church, *ristras* (strings) of scarlet chile peppers overhanging the walls of village houses and barns, tumbleweeds piled against a fence enclosing longhorn cattle, dry heat shimmering over the desert sand, the soft lights of *luminiaries* at twilight. Glimpses of the Southwest are unusual experiences of sometimes very ordinary things that mark a place in the memory. Recalled, these glimpses open the gates of the mind to a flood of sensual images.

America's Southwest is still peopled with many Indians, descendants of the original inhabitants of this magical land. Such tribes as the Hopi, Navajo, Pima, Pueblo, Apache, Comanche, Cheyenne and Cherokee have made their homes here. Those who remain are mainly farmers and herders on reservations, where they live much as their ancestors did centuries ago. Others live in cities and industrial towns where they pursue their lives as part of the modern world.

Spanish-Americans live here as well, in small farming communities, in secluded foothill valleys and in the growing cities. In the villages they raise sheep, goats and poultry and grow fruits and vegetables, among them the ever-present chile peppers. Anglo-Americans of European and Canadian descent live in the cities and farms of the Southwest as well, working in the burgeoning industries and trades.

The Southwest has much to offer, from such exotic foods as piñon nuts, prickly-pear jam, cactus candy and enchiladas, to exquisitely crafted silver and turquoise jewelry. Side by side with the abandoned stores of the old cowboy towns are emporia offering ten-gallon hats and handmade cowboy boots. Where in the daytime an outdoor concert entertains music-lovers, at night a fiesta enthralls with its whirling colors, wafting scents and lively music.

The Southwest is an amalgamation of diverse and colorful cultures and places, people and events. Both distinctive in its own right and part of the greater whole that is America, the Southwest is one of the country's greatest regional treasures.

105 *The Jeff Haskell Trio performs in a festival concert in the mall in Scottsdale, Arizona. Playing outdoors is a way of life for the people of the southwestern states, and informality is a prerequisite for most of them.*

106/107 *Cowboys and their cattle on the Whitehead Ranch in Arizona. Cattle is the most important farm crop in Arizona, accounting for 40 percent of the value of all farm crops produced, but less than two percent of the land is used for farming.*

108 *The mountain lion (or cougar, panther, puma),which once ranged across the continent, is now limited mostly to western states. Once considered a pest by ranchers, the endangered cougar is now receiving protection from conservation officers.*

109 *Steep trails can be found in Randolph Canyon in the Superstition Wilderness. Riding horses along trails such as these is a favorite outdoor activity in the great Southwest.*

110/111 *A cattle drive on an Arizona ranch.*

112 A surrealistic view in the Scottsdale Mall in
Arizona at dusk.

113 Palms cast their shadows on the West Facade
of the Scottsdale Center for the Arts in Arizona.
This multipurpose community arts facility offers
more than 800 public events annually—dance,
theater, piano recitals, jazz, classic films,
Shakespeare and culinary and arts festivals.

114 The mission church of San Xavier del Bac, 'The White Dove of the Desert,' near Tucson, Arizona. Father Kino, the Jesuit who sought to convert the Pimas and other Indians, founded the mission in 1700, and the church was built between 1783 and 1797.

115 The old Lee Lumber Company building in Oatman, Arizona—a relic with its corrugated iron front.

116/117 A time exposure of automobile headlights and taillights along the Bee-line Highway (US Route 87) between Phoenix and Payson, Arizona.

118 A detail from a blanket made by the Huichol Indians and exhibited at the Friends of Mexico Art Festival in Arizona.

119 A resident of the Taos Pueblo near Taos, New Mexico. The pueblo includes a double apartment house; the north building is four stories high, and the south is two stories high. Small buildings and corrals are scattered among these impressive Indian architectural masterpieces.

120 Montezuma's Castle near Camp Verde, Arizona.

121 Passageways in the Pueblo Bonito in Chaco Canyon National Park in New Mexico. Chaco Canyon was a major center of Pueblo Indian culture from about 900 to 1150 AD. It was the center of a vast, complex and independent civilization in the American Southwest.

122/123 Zuni dancers from New Mexico. The Zuni Pueblo is located 41 miles south of Gallup, and is alleged to be one of Coronado's 'Seven Cities of Gold.' The pueblo is built mainly of stone and most of it is one story high. The Shalako dance, usually held in late November or early December, is one of the best known and most spectacular of Indian ceremonies.

124 *A roadside chili stand is a welcoming sight.*

125 *Chilies on a string and ready for sale.*